THE PITTSBURGH STEELERS

Sloan MacRae

PowerKiDS press

New York

Published in 2010 by The Rosen Publishing Group, Inc.
29 East 21st Street, New York, NY 10010

First Edition

Editor: Amelie von Zumbusch
Book Design: Greg Tucker
Photo Researcher: Jessica Gerweck

Photo Credits: Cover (Jerome Bettis), pp. 17, 22 (bottom) Ron Vesely/Getty Images; cover (Terry Bradshaw) Scott Cunningham/Getty Images; cover (Troy Polamalu), p. 19 Joe Robbins/Getty Images; cover (background), p. 7 Shutterstock.com; p. 5 Al Bello/Getty Images; p. 9 Streeter Lecka/Getty Images; p. 11 Football Hall of Fame/NFL/Getty Images; p. 13 © Bettmann/Corbis; pp. 15, 22 (bottom) Sylvia Allen/NFL/Getty Images; p. 21 Chris Graythen/Getty Images.

Library of Congress Cataloging-in-Publication Data

MacRae, Sloan.
  The Pittsburgh Steelers / Sloan MacRae. — 1st ed.
      p. cm. — (America's greatest teams)
  Includes index.
  ISBN 978-1-4042-8131-8 (library binding) — ISBN 978-1-4358-3396-8 (pbk.) — ISBN 978-1-4358-3397-5 (6-pack)
  1. Pittsburgh Steelers (Football team)—History—Juvenile literature. I. Title.
  GV956.P57M34 2010
  796.332'640974886—dc22
                                    2009008641

Manufactured in the United States of America

CPSIA Compliance Information: Batch #WR904211PK: For Further Information contact Rosen Publishing, New York, New York at 1-800-237-9932

CONTENTS

TOUGH AS STEEL 4

THE BIG KETCHUP BOTTLE 6

THE TERRIBLE TOWEL 8

THE PITTSBURGH PIRATES 10

THE STEAGLES AND THE CARPETS 12

THE STEEL CURTAIN 14

HOMETOWN HERO 16

ONE FOR THE THUMB 18

ONE FOR THE OTHER THUMB 20

PITTSBURGH STEELERS TIMELINE 22

GLOSSARY 23

INDEX 24

WEB SITES 24

TOUGH AS STEEL

Football is a **tough** game, and football players have to be tough. The Pittsburgh Steelers might not always be the flashiest players, but they are known for their toughness. The Steelers are famous for their strong **defense** and powerful **running backs**. In 2009, this tough team broke the record for the number of Super Bowl wins.

Some of the greatest players in the history of the National Football League, or NFL, have been Pittsburgh Steelers. No **quarterback** has more Super Bowl rings than Terry Bradshaw. Superstars such as Joe Greene, Jack Lambert, Troy Polamalu, and James Harrison have made the Steelers' defense famous around the world.

The record-breaking 2008 Steelers had a strong defense. It included Deshea Townsend (left), James Harrison (middle), and Ike Taylor (right).

THE BIG KETCHUP BOTTLE

The Steelers play at Heinz Field. The **stadium** gets its name from Heinz, a famous Pittsburgh company that makes ketchup. Some football fans call Heinz Field the Big Ketchup Bottle.

The team's **logo** is made up of sparklike shapes in three colors. It is based on the logo of the American Iron and Steel Institute. The team chose this logo because Pittsburgh was once known for its steel mills. Black and gold are the **official** colors of the city of Pittsburgh. However, they are better known as the colors of the Steelers. The Steelers' success is the reason Pittsburgh's baseball and hockey teams wear the same colors.

Heinz Field is on the Ohio River. It sits very near the place where the Allegheny River and Monongahela River meet to form the Ohio.

THE TERRIBLE TOWEL

The Rooney family has always been the Steelers' main owner. The Rooneys and the Steelers are proud **representatives** of Pittsburgh. In the 1970s, many people in Pittsburgh lost their jobs when the steel mills went out of business. The Steelers gave them hope in tough times.

The Steelers are one of the best-loved teams in all of American sports. In fact, when the Steelers travel to other stadiums, they often have more fans than the home teams. You can tell if Steelers fans are at a game because they wave yellow towels, known as Terrible Towels. The Terrible Towel was invented by a Pittsburgh sports **broadcaster**, named Myron Cope.

The Terrible Towel has become famous across the United States. Steelers fans first waved their Terrible Towels during the play-offs for the 1975 season.

9

THE PITTSBURGH PIRATES

The Steelers are one of the oldest NFL teams. In 1933, businessman Art Rooney formed a new football team in Pittsburgh. The city had a well-liked baseball team called the Pirates, so Rooney named his football team the Pittsburgh Pirates. In 1940, Rooney changed his team's name to the Steelers. The team has been known as the Steelers ever since.

The Pittsburgh Steelers struggled for many years, even though the team had great players. One of the greatest Pittsburgh players of the 1930s was Byron White. White loved football, but he decided to do something else with his life. In time, he became a Supreme Court justice.

Byron White, seen here, was known as Whizzer White because he was so fast. White played for Pittsburgh during the 1938 season.

THE STEAGLES AND THE CARPETS

In the early 1940s, football teams across the United States had trouble finding enough players. Many players had left the game to serve in World War II. Some years, the Steelers did not have enough players to field a whole team. In 1943, the Steelers combined with the Philadelphia Eagles to become one team. They were nicknamed the Steagles.

The Steelers had to join forces with the Chicago Cardinals in 1944. The combined team was called the Card-Pitt. Sadly, the Pittsburgh-Chicago team did not win a single game in the regular season. People nicknamed them the Carpets because other teams walked all over them.

Forbes Field was home to Pittsburgh's NFL team until 1963. Even when the Steelers joined with other teams in the 1940s, they played some games here.

THE STEEL CURTAIN

The Steelers struggled during the 1950s and 1960s. Then, Chuck Noll became their head coach for the 1969 season. He turned the team around. Noll **drafted** new young players who, in time, became stars. Many sports fans agree that the Steelers' draft class of 1974 was the best ever.

In the 1970s, the Steelers became the first team to win four Super Bowls. They are still the only team to win four Super Bowls in only six years. The Steelers' **offense** was led by quarterback Terry Bradshaw, running back Franco Harris, and **wide receivers** Lynn Swann and John Stallworth. Joe Greene, Jack Lambert, and Mel Blount led the "Steel Curtain" defense.

In 1975, the Steelers appeared in, and won, their first Super Bowl. Franco Harris (center) was named the game's most valuable player, or MVP.

15

HOMETOWN HERO

The superstars of the Steelers started to **retire** in the 1980s. The team began to struggle for the first time in years. Pittsburgh often had good players, but the team would not win another Super Bowl for 26 years.

In 1992, Chuck Noll retired. Bill Cowher became the next head coach. Cowher was a long-time Steelers fan because he had grown up near Pittsburgh. The Steelers reached the **postseason** in each of Cowher's first six years with the team. They made it to the Super Bowl in 1996, but they lost to the Dallas Cowboys. It was the first Super Bowl the Steelers ever lost.

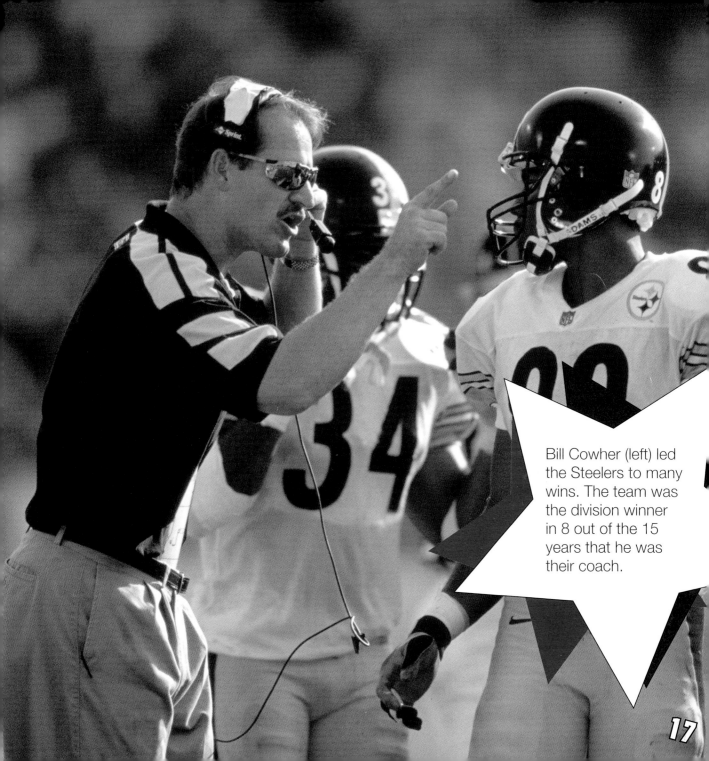

Bill Cowher (left) led the Steelers to many wins. The team was the division winner in 8 out of the 15 years that he was their coach.

ONE FOR THE THUMB

The Steelers returned to greatness under Cowher's leadership. Star running back Jerome Bettis and wide receiver Hines Ward became team leaders. The Steelers also added Troy Polamalu. Polamalu is known both for his long hair and for being one of the NFL's fastest defensive players.

The Steelers teams in the late 1990s and early 2000s were often good. However, they lacked a star quarterback. In 2004, they got one in Ben Roethlisberger. Roethlisberger and the Steelers beat the Seattle Seahawks in the 2006 Super Bowl. The Steelers finally had a fifth Super Bowl ring, or, as they said, "one for the thumb."

Defensive Steelers players, such as Ike Taylor (left) and Troy Polamalu (right), played a big part in the team's success in the 2000s.

ONE FOR THE OTHER THUMB

The Steelers are still known for their toughness. **Linebacker** James Harrison was named Defensive Player of the Year in 2008. That same season, Roethlisberger proved that he was one of the NFL's toughest quarterbacks around when he played well against another tough team, the Baltimore Ravens.

Mike Tomlin became the Steelers' coach in 2007. He led the team to the Super Bowl in just his second season. The 2009 Super Bowl was a close game. The Steelers beat the Arizona Cardinals thanks to plays by Roethlisberger, Harrison, and wide receiver Santonio Holmes. The Steelers became the first team to win six Super Bowls. Their fans know that they are tough enough to win more.

A proud Santonio Holmes (middle) and Ben Roethlisberger (right) held up the Vince Lombardi Trophy after the 2009 Super Bowl.

PITTSBURGH STEELERS TIMELINE

1933
Art Rooney founds a football team called the Pittsburgh Pirates.

1940
The Pittsburgh Pirates change their name to the Pittsburgh Steelers.

1947
The Steelers make the play-offs for the first time.

1969
Chuck Noll becomes the coach of the Steelers.

1972
Franco Harris makes a catch that becomes known as the Immaculate Reception. This is the most famous play in Steelers history.

1975
The Steelers win their first Super Bowl against the Minnesota Vikings.

1980
The Steelers win their fourth Super Bowl in six years.

1992
Chuck Noll retires, and Bill Cowher (left) becomes the Steelers' coach.

2009
Mike Tomlin becomes the youngest coach to lead his team to the Super Bowl.

GLOSSARY

BROADCASTER (BROD-kas-ter) Someone who speaks on TV or the radio.

DEFENSE (DEE-fents) The part of a team that tries to stop another team from scoring.

DRAFTED (DRAFT-ed) Selected people for a special purpose.

LINEBACKER (LYN-ba-ker) A player who lines up behind the other defensive players and tries to stop the other team's offense.

LOGO (LOH-goh) The pictures or words that stand for a team or company.

OFFENSE (AH-fents) The part of a team that tries to score points in a game.

OFFICIAL (uh-FIH-shul) Formal or legal.

POSTSEASON (pohst-SEE-zun) Games played after the regular season.

QUARTERBACK (KWAHR-ter-bak) The football player who directs a team's plays.

REPRESENTATIVES (reh-prih-ZEN-tuh-tivz) People chosen to speak for others.

RETIRE (rih-TY-ur) To give up an office or job.

RUNNING BACKS (RUN-ing BAKS) Football players who run with the ball, block players from the other team, and sometimes catch the ball.

STADIUM (STAY-dee-um) A place where sports are played.

TOUGH (TUF) Strong or hard.

WIDE RECEIVERS (WYD rih-SEE-verz) Football players who run down the field and catch the ball.

INDEX

B
Bradshaw, Terry, 4, 14

C
Cowher, Bill, 16, 18

D
defense, 4, 14

F
fan(s), 6, 8, 14, 16, 20
football, 4, 10

G
game(s), 4, 8, 12, 20
Greene, Joe, 4, 14

H
Harrison, James, 4, 20

L
Lambert, Jack, 4, 14
logo, 6

N
Noll, Chuck, 14, 16, 22

O
offense, 14

P
player(s), 4, 10, 12, 14, 16, 18, 20

Polamalu, Troy, 4, 18
postseason, 16

Q
quarterback(s), 4, 18, 20

R
record, 4
representatives, 8
ring(s), 4, 18
Roethlisberger, Ben, 18, 20
running backs, 4

S
stadium(s), 6, 8
Super Bowl wins, 4

WEB SITES

Due to the changing nature of Internet links, PowerKids Press has developed an online list of Web sites related to the subject of this book. This site is updated regularly. Please use this link to access the list:
www.powerkidslinks.com/teams/steeler/